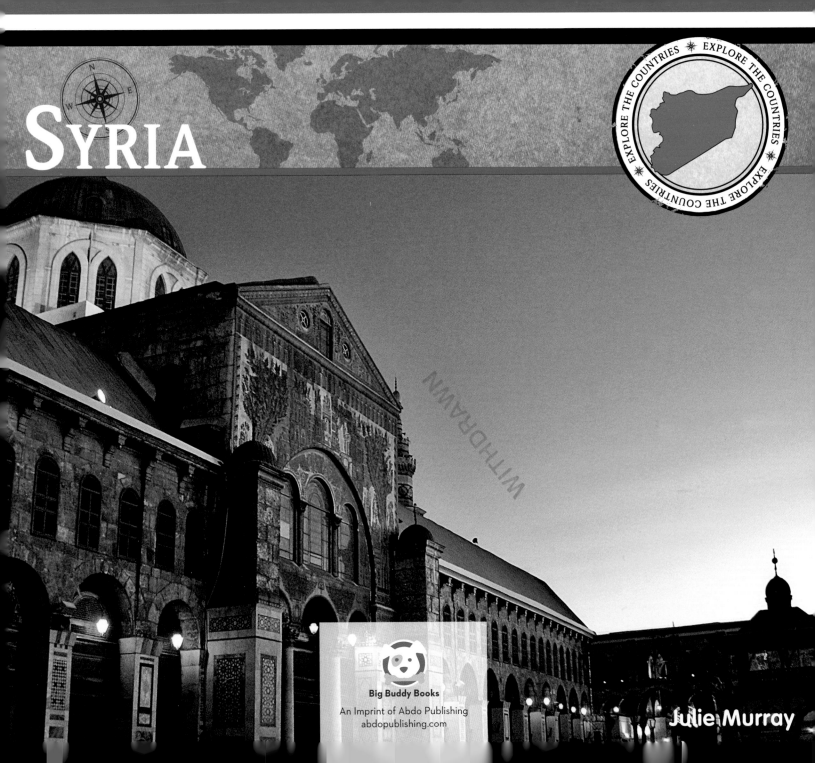

SYRIA

Big Buddy Books
An Imprint of Abdo Publishing
abdopublishing.com

Julie Murray

abdopublishing.com

Published by Abdo Publishing, a division of ABDO, PO Box 398166, Minneapolis, Minnesota 55439.
Copyright © 2018 by Abdo Consulting Group, Inc. International copyrights reserved in all countries. No part of this book may be reproduced in any form without written permission from the publisher. Big Buddy Books™ is a trademark and logo of Abdo Publishing.

Printed in the United States of America, North Mankato, Minnesota.
052017
092017

Cover Photo: ©iStockphoto.com.
Interior Photos: age fotostock/Alamy Stock Photo (p. 9); Art of Food/Alamy Stock Photo (p. 27); ASSOCIATED PRESS (p. 17); Ryan Rodrick Beiler/Alamy Stock Photo (p. 29); bilwissedition Ltd. & Co. KG/Alamy Stock Photo (p. 16); Buiten-Beeld/Alamy Stock Photo (p. 21); Nigel Cattlin/Alamy Stock Photo (p. 23); Luis Dafos/Alamy Stock Photo (p. 5); De Agostini Picture Library/Granger, NYC -- All rights reserved. (p. 13); Eddie Gerald/Alamy Stock Photo (p. 25); richard harvey/Alamy Stock Photo (p. 15); Peter Horree/Alamy Stock Photo (p. 35); INTERFOTO/Alamy Stock Photo (p. 31); ©iStockphoto.com (pp. 23, 34, 35, 38); John Warburton-Lee Photography/Alamy Stock Photo (p. 35); Nick Ledger/Alamy Stock Photo (p. 37); PA Images/Alamy Stock Photo (p. 33); Miguel Pereira/Alamy Stock Photo (p. 19); REUTERS/Alamy Stock Photo (p. 11); Robert Preston Photography/Alamy Stock Photo (p. 34); Steve Allen Travel Photography/Alamy Stock Photo (p. 19); Tengku Mohd Yusof/Alamy Stock Photo (p. 11).

Coordinating Series Editor: Tamara L. Britton
Editor: Katie Lajiness
Graphic Design: Taylor Higgins, Keely McKernan

Country population and area figures taken from the CIA World Factbook.

Publisher's Cataloging-in-Publication Data

Names: Murray, Julie, 1969- , author.
Title: Syria / by Julie Murray.
Description: Minneapolis, MN : Abdo Publishing, 2018. | Series: Explore the countries | Includes bibliographical references and index.
Identifiers: LCCN 2016962353 | ISBN 9781532110528 (lib. bdg.) | ISBN 9781680788372 (ebook)
Subjects: LCSH: Syria--Juvenile literature.
Classification: DDC 956.91--dc23
LC record available at http://lccn.loc.gov/2016962353

SYRIA

CONTENTS

AROUND THE WORLD

Our world has many countries. Each country has beautiful land. It has its own rich history. And, the people have their own languages and ways of life.

Syria is a country in Asia. What do you know about Syria? Let's learn more about this place and its story!

Did You Know?

Arabic is the official language in Syria.

Syrian men perform traditional dances to honor their culture.

SAY IT

Syria
SIHR- ee-uh

Passport to Syria

Syria is located in a part of the world known as the Middle East. Five countries border Syria. The Mediterranean Sea is to the west.

The country's total area is 71,498 square miles (185,180 sq km). More than 17 million people live there.

Did You Know?

Syria is about the size of Washington State.

WHERE IN THE WORLD?

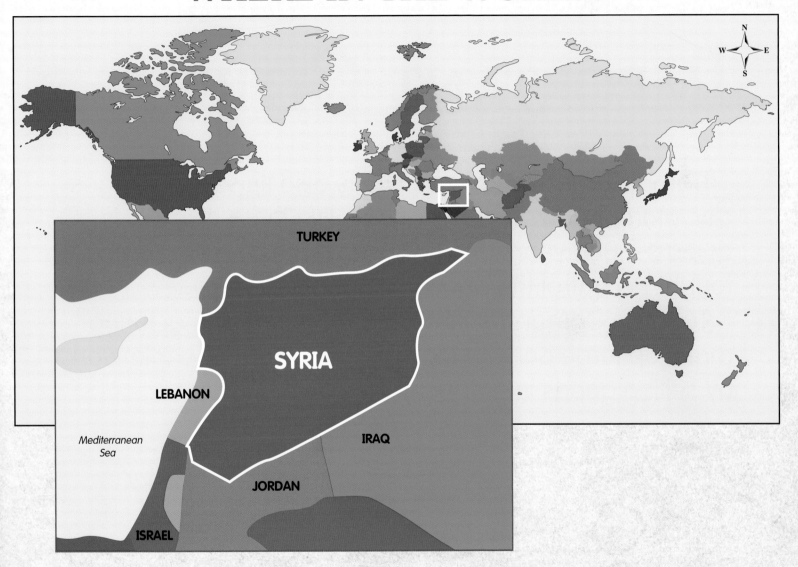

Important Cities

Damascus is Syria's **capital**. It is also its second-largest city. More than 2.5 million people live there. The city is at least 5,000 years old. In ancient times, many groups fought to control the city and its trade.

Today in Damascus, government and manufacturing make up large parts of the **economy**. Some people work by selling goods in outdoor markets.

SAY IT

Damascus
duh-MAS-kuhs

SYRIA

•Aleppo

• Homs

★ Damascus

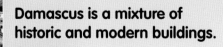

Damascus is a mixture of historic and modern buildings.

Syria's largest city is Aleppo. More than 3.5 million live there. Aleppo is known for its narrow streets and outdoor markets. Since 2011, much of Aleppo has been destroyed in Syria's **civil war**. Thousands of people have left the city in search of safety.

Homs is Syria's third-largest city. About 1.6 million people call it home. Homs connects Syria's cities to the Mediterranean coast. The area's rich soil makes Homs a major farming area.

> ## SAY IT
>
> **Aleppo**
> *uh-LEH-poh*
>
> **Homs**
> *HAWMZ*

Aleppo's Al-Madina Souq market dates back to the 1300s. Shops there sell ceramics, food, soaps, and cloth.

The Syrian civil war began in Homs. People there started to question the government and its leaders.

SYRIA IN HISTORY

Syria has one of the oldest **cultures** in the world. People have lived in what is now Syria since at least 8,000 BC. Throughout history, many kingdoms took over the land. Eventually it was ruled by the **Ottoman Empire**.

In 1920, France took over Syria. Syria gained its independence in 1946. However, a series of military leaders took over the government. In 1961, Syria became an independent state again.

Traders in ancient Syria traveled by land and sea to deliver goods to Africa, Asia, and Europe.

13

In the 1980s, Syria's **economy** began to slow. The population continued to grow despite a **drought**. Dishonest leaders used their power to hurt the Syrian people.

Some people fought back against the government. A **civil war** began in 2011. As of 2016, there is still no peace for the people. And, Syria continues to fight with Israel over land between the two countries.

During the civil war, entire neighborhoods in Aleppo were destroyed. Two years after the war began, almost half of the city was in ruins.

TIMELINE

332 BC

Alexander the Great ruled
over what is now Syria.

1918

Arab troops captured
Damascus and ended 400
years of **Ottoman** rule.

AD **1831**

Egyptian prince Ibrahim
Pasha took over Syria. He
ruled for nearly ten years.

1967

Israel took land called the Golan Heights from Syria. This started the Six Day War.

2000

President Hafez al-Assad died. His second son, Bashar, took over.

2015

After four years of fighting, the Syrian Army took back control of Homs from the **rebels**.

An Important Symbol

Syria's flag was first adopted in 1958. The flag has red, white, and black stripes. There are two green stars on the white stripe.

The country is a **republic**. The president is the head of state. However, he or she acts with absolute power. The prime minister is the head of government.

Syria is divided into 14 provinces. This is a large section within a country, like a state.

SAY IT

Bashar al-Assad
bah-SHAW ahl-ah-SAHD

In the past, Syria has had different flags. Syria's current flag was adopted in 1980.

Bashar al-Assad became president in 2000. He came into power after his father and older brother died.

ACROSS THE LAND

Syria has coastlines, mountains, plains, and valleys. High temperatures cause dust storms and **droughts**. From 2006 to 2011, Syria had the worst drought in its history.

 Did You Know?

In January, the average temperature is about 48°F (9°C). In July, it is about 81°F (27°C).

At 9,232 feet (2,814 m) high, Mount Hermon is Syria's highest peak.

21

Throughout Syria, olive trees, grapevines, apricot trees, oaks, and poplars are common. Fir trees grow in the mountains. Date palms are found in the valleys.

Few wild animals live in Syria. Animals such as badgers, foxes, hyenas, and wolves live in far-off areas. Chameleons, lizards, and vipers are common in the desert.

Forests make up only a small amount of the country's total area. They are mostly found in the Al-Ansariyyah Mountains.

Syria is home to 10,000 different kinds of locusts.

Earning a Living

Syria's **civil war** has slowed its **economy**. But many Syrians still work in banking, government, health care, and transportation. Some manufacture cars, clothes, food, or medicine. Others grow crops such barley, cotton, and wheat. They also raise cattle, chickens, and sheep.

In Syria, 180,000 barrels of oil can be produced in one day.

LIFE IN SYRIA

Different groups of people were taken in when Syria separated from the **Ottoman Empire**. So, Syria has a rich **cultural** history.

In Syria, family is very important. People often visit a family member's home for meals. These are made with a wide range of ingredients. Garlic, lemon, onions, and spices are often used.

Did You Know?

In Syria, basic education is mandatory for children ages 6 to 14.

A common dish in Syria is fish with rice, lemons, and tomatoes with pita bread.

Like many Middle Eastern countries, soccer is a popular sport in Syria. There are sports stadiums in Aleppo and Damascus.

Most people in Syria are **Muslim**. The two major groups are Sunni and Shia. More than 75 percent of the Muslims are Sunnis. Smaller religious populations also live in Syria.

The Great Mosque of Damascus is the oldest surviving stone mosque. It was built in the early 700s. Today, people still gather there to pray.

FAMOUS FACES

Many talented people are from Syria. Adonis is a Syrian-Lebanese poet. He was born in western Syria on January 1, 1930.

At age 14, he recited a poem to the Syrian president. The president was impressed. He helped send Adonis to a French high school and Damascus University.

During the 1960s, Adonis helped create a new form of **Arabic** poetry. Today, Adonis is considered one of the greatest Arab poets of all time.

SAY IT
Adonis
uh-DAH-nuhs

Adonis has won poetry awards such as the Syria-Lebanon Best Poet Award.

Ghada Shouaa is a Syrian Olympian. Shouaa was born September 10, 1973, in Mahardah, Syria. She **competed** in the **heptathlon**. This is a track and field sport with seven events.

In 1991, Shouaa competed in the world **championships** in Tokyo, Japan. That year, Shouaa won the silver medal at the Asian Games.

Then, she competed in three straight Olympics. At the 1996 games, Shouaa won Syria's first gold medal. She holds the fifth-best heptathlon score in history.

SAY IT

Ghada Shouaa
GAHD-ah SHOO-ah

At the 1996 Olympics, Shouaa won with a total score of 6,780 points. She became a role model for other Arab athletes.

TOUR BOOK

Imagine traveling to Syria! Here are some places you could go and things you could do.

Visit

The city of Bosra is home to ancient ruins. A Roman theater from the 100s still stands.

See

The ancient city of Damascus was one of the first cities in the Middle East. See more than 125 monuments from throughout history.

 # Explore

The ruins of the Dead Cities still feature old buildings and ancient pyramids.

 # Discover

Tartus is on the shores of the Mediterranean Sea. People ride jet skis in this beautiful setting.

 # Ride

Palmyra was an ancient city. Take a camel ride across the desert and see the ruins.

A Great Country

The story of Syria is important to our world. Syria is a land of ancient ruins and stunning coastlines. It is a country of people who are hoping to live in peace.

The people and places that make up Syria offer something special. They help make the world a more beautiful, interesting place.

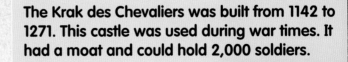

The Krak des Chevaliers was built from 1142 to 1271. This castle was used during war times. It had a moat and could hold 2,000 soldiers.

SYRIA UP CLOSE

Official Name:
Syrian Arab Republic

Flag:

Population (rank): 17,185,170
(July 2016 est.)
(66th most-populated country)

Total Area (rank): 71,498 square miles
(89th largest country)

Capital: Damascus

Official Language: Arabic

Currency: Syrian pound

Form of Government: Republic

National Anthem: "Humat ad-Diyar"
("Guardians of the Homeland")

IMPORTANT WORDS

Arab of or relating to a member of the peoples who are originally from the Arabian Peninsula and who now live mostly in the Middle East and northern Africa. Something Arabic relates to Arab people or culture or the Arabic language.

capital a city where government leaders meet.

championship a game, a match, or a race to find a first-place winner.

civil war a war between groups in the same country.

compete to take part in a contest between two or more persons or groups.

culture (KUHL-chuhr) the arts, beliefs, and ways of life of a group of people.

drought (DRAUT) a long period of dry weather.

economy the way that a country produces, sells, and buys goods and services.

heptathlon a composite contest for female athletes that consists of the 100-meter hurdles, the high jump, the shot put, the 200-meter dash, the long jump, the javelin throw, and the 800-meter run.

Muslim a person who practices Islam, which is a religion based on a belief in Allah as God and Muhammad as his prophet.

Ottoman Empire an empire created by Turkish tribes in Asia that grew to be one of the most powerful states in the world during the 1400s and 1500s.

rebel a person who resists authority.

republic a government in which the people choose the leader.

WEBSITES

To learn more about Explore the Countries, visit **abdobooklinks.com**. These links are routinely monitored and updated to provide the most current information available.

INDEX

31901061101061